CW00348767

Who Am I?

ANGELA REITH

WHO
AM I?

Discovering your personality
with the Enneagram

LION
Giftlines

Published by
Lion Publishing plc
Sandy Lane West, Oxford, England
www.lion-publishing.co.uk
ISBN 0 7459 4066 8

First edition 1999
10 9 8 7 6 5 4 3 2 1 0

Acknowledgments

We would like to thank all those who have given us permission to include material in
this book. Every effort has been made to trace and acknowledge copyright holders of
all the quotations in this book. We apologize for any errors or omissions that may remain,
and would ask those concerned to contact the publishers, who will ensure that full
acknowledgment is made in the future.

All illustrations conceptualized by Angela Reith.

Page 43: Extracts taken from *The Cloud of Unknowing and the Book of Privy Counselling*,
edited by William Johnstone (New York: Image Books, Doubleday and Co., Inc., 1973) and
The Little Prince by Antoine De Saint-Exupery, translated by Katherine Woods (New York:
Reynal and Hitchcok, 1943).

The following works have been invaluable in writing this book:

The Enneagram and Prayer: Discovering our true selves before God, Barbara Metz and Jon Burchill
The Enneagram Made Easy: Discover the 9 types of people, Renee Baron and Elizabeth Wagele
The Enneagram: Understanding yourself and the others in your life, Helen Palmer

A catalogue record for this book is available
from the British Library

Typeset in 9/11 Goudy Old Style
Printed and bound in Singapore

Contents

Who am I?

9. It's lovely to be here together like this

1- This Mouton-Rothschild 1982 ought to be just right

3. It's a success! Worth the days of preparation

8 - Turn up the music!

6- Did I remember to lock the front door? -

4. I wish someone would talk to me...

2. Can I get you something to eat?

7. I could dance all night!

5. 'The Ancient Etruscans.' Hmm- interesting

Introduction
What is the Enneagram?

The Enneagram is an established method of understanding distinctive human qualities and characteristics. It operates by grouping individuals into nine broad personality types. Understanding your personality type can give you valuable insights into why you do things and the ways in which you react to situations. This can help you to move towards better relationships with family, friends and colleagues.

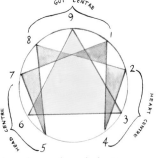

The exact origin of the Enneagram is not known, but it is believed to have been developed in the East and used by Christian mystics more than 1,500 years ago. It was brought to the West in the 1920s by the Russian spiritual teacher and psychologist G.I. Gurdjieff. The word Enneagram (pronounced 'any-a-gram') is derived from the Greek words *ennea* ('nine') and *grammos* ('drawing').

The Enneagram is traditionally represented by a circle with nine points on its circumference. Each point is given a number which corresponds to one of the nine personality types.

Each type of personality is in relationship with two other types; these relationships are represented on the circle by lines which link them in a particular pattern (see page 56).

Each personality type is also influenced by the types on each side of it on the circle. These are called the 'wings'.

Finally, the nine types are grouped together into three 'centres': the 'heart' or 'feeling' centre, the 'head' or 'thinking' centre and the 'gut' or 'instinctive' centre. The centre is where a person's deepest reactions come from; understanding this can help you to have more choice about how you live.

As the diagram shows, the three centres are ruled by three problem areas: image, fear and anger. Each personality type also has a specific problem or 'core issue' to deal with: greed, fear, gluttony, lust, sloth, anger, pride, deceit and envy.

'Like the sea, the Enneagram is shallow enough for the most timid of bathers, and yet deep enough for an ocean liner.'

Simon Parke

Understanding your personality

As we go through life, we take with us our personality and the many influences we have received throughout our childhood.

Along the way life throws good and bad things at us and we react as best we can...

And because we do not know much about ourselves, we often struggle to make sense of who we are and why we react in certain ways...

As a result, we can make life hard for ourselves and others.

The Enneagram can be like an honest friend, a mirror, revealing our failings so that we can change for the better. It can open up to us possibilities we never dreamed of.

9

When we know more about ourselves, we can learn to accept our weaknesses, and have more choice in avoiding the pitfalls in our personalities. When we know more about others, we can learn to respect and value their differences, and so live more peaceably with them.

On discovering the insights that the Enneagram gives, it is tempting to categorize ourselves and our friends and family in a way that is unhelpful. Putting people in boxes – however enlightened – does not do justice to their complexity as human beings. Getting locked into the belief that we are a certain personality type can also prevent us from making positive changes. The Enneagram is a powerful tool to help you understand yourself better, but it is only a tool: it is not the whole truth.

The journey begins

The next few pages will help you to work out your personality type. You can then go on to read about it in more detail: the positive and negative points; how you relate to others; work and activities which might suit you, and some pointers towards learning and growing.

Subsequent chapters take a look at two topics that are of interest to us all: our intimate relationships and our spirituality.

Of course, a book of this size will only give you the most basic information about the Enneagram. If you wish to find out more, there is a book-list for further reading on page 64.

Finding your number

On the next few pages you will find a series of statements relating to each of the nine Enneagram personality types. Work through them all, ticking the boxes next to the phrases you can hear yourself saying. There are no right or wrong answers. Be as honest as possible, even if you seem to be contradicting yourself here and there. When you have finished, see which number has the most ticked boxes. That number is most likely to be your personality type.

If the ticks are more or less even for some numbers, think about where your deepest reactions stem from (your 'centre') and about your weaknesses. These may help you to decide.

Then you can turn to the section which focuses on your number and discover more about your personality type.

*'The Enneagram is about exposing
compulsions and releasing gifts;
it is concerned with accurate
diagnosis and change to health.'*

Simon Parke

Number One: *The Perfectionist*

- [ ] I like to be orderly
- [ ] I prefer people to keep the rules
- [ ] I hate people to be late
- [ ] I hang on to resentment
- [ ] I'm practical and realistic
- [ ] I feel guilty about relaxing
- [ ] I dread criticism and judgment
- [ ] Things are either right or wrong
- [ ] I compare myself with others
- [ ] I'm dependable – mostly
- [ ] Details are important
- [ ] I don't often think about what I want

- [ ] I feel that I'm right
- [ ] Spontaneity is hard
- [ ] I dot the 'i's and cross the 't's
- [ ] I feel guilty when I don't get enough done
- [ ] I have high ideals
- [ ] Jealousy makes me afraid and competitive
- [ ] I think hard before spending
- [ ] Truth and justice are important
- [ ] I worry a great deal
- [ ] Anger isn't good or right
- [ ] I love doing a job well
- [ ] I'm afraid of making mistakes

Number Two: *The Helper*

- [ ] Relationships are very important
- [ ] My friends need me
- [ ] I'm not sure who is the real me
- [ ] I want to be seen as sexy, but not to have sex
- [ ] Personal freedom is important
- [ ] I like to be asked for advice
- [ ] I adapt to whoever I'm with
- [ ] It's hard to act independently of others
- [ ] I expect to receive in return for my help
- [ ] It's exciting to win someone's love
- [ ] I feel hurt if I don't get the closeness I need
- [ ] I want approval from people

- [ ] I hide my needs from others
- [ ] I'm not sure what my needs are
- [ ] I like being with 'important' or 'inspired' people
- [ ] I dislike feeling controlled by others' needs
- [ ] I'm afraid to look inside myself
- [ ] I do things to please others
- [ ] If I say what I need I'll be rejected
- [ ] I get tired of being the one who gives
- [ ] I'm afraid of intimacy
- [ ] I'm the power behind the throne
- [ ] I'm easily hurt by criticism
- [ ] People don't appreciate me enough

Number Three: *The Achiever*

- [ ] I'm efficient
- [ ] I value achievement
- [ ] I'm loved for what I achieve
- [ ] I often don't know what I feel
- [ ] Personal feelings can interfere with the job
- [ ] Public image is important
- [ ] I don't like wasting time
- [ ] I like doing several things at once
- [ ] I achieve good things
- [ ] I like setting the rules
- [ ] I have great enthusiasm
- [ ] I don't think much before I act
- [ ] I'm competitive

- [ ] I like to feel financially secure
- [ ] I focus on the positive
- [ ] It's important to get the job done
- [ ] I like lots of approval
- [ ] I don't talk about my personal life
- [ ] I'm very focused
- [ ] My public image is the real me
- [ ] I want respect from others
- [ ] I can easily make people trust me
- [ ] I get the best out of people
- [ ] I work hard
- [ ] I avoid negative people

Number Four: *The Romantic*

- Love will bring me happiness
- My feelings go up and down
- Feelings help me to make decisions
- I have very dark moods
- I often feel a sense of loss
- I enjoy feeling sad or melancholic
- Things that are easy to get aren't worth having
- I like deep relationships
- I need to understand myself
- I'm different; I don't belong
- I want intimacy
- People say I'm too intense
- I'm afraid of intimacy
- I like to be sought out

- Other people's idiosyncrasies annoy me
- I don't want to be ordinary
- I look for integrity in others
- I focus on the past or future, not the present
- I often want more than I have
- I'm sensitive to the feelings of others
- I'm a good support in a crisis
- I quickly focus on the negative
- Nobody can ever understand me
- I'm not governed by fashion
- It hurts if someone forgets or criticizes me
- I don't like being controlled

Number Five: *The Observer*

- [ ] I sometimes unplug the phone
- [ ] It's hard to ask for what I need
- [ ] I often don't know what I feel
- [ ] Self-control is a good thing
- [ ] I don't like over-dramatic people
- [ ] On my own, I'm freer to feel emotion
- [ ] I compartmentalize my life
- [ ] I prefer friends who share my expertise
- [ ] My friends don't know each other
- [ ] I like life to be predictable
- [ ] I like systems explaining how people work
- [ ] I like to have special knowledge

- [ ] I'd rather observe than join in
- [ ] I'm good at analysing objectively
- [ ] I'm a loner
- [ ] I like to know who'll be at the dinner party
- [ ] I'd rather not go to the dinner party
- [ ] I enjoy things in retrospect
- [ ] I'm afraid of intimacy
- [ ] I don't like having a fuss made of me
- [ ] I sometimes watch myself living
- [ ] I'm good at doing without
- [ ] I don't like getting involved
- [ ] I sometimes feel superior to others
- [ ] I can lose myself for hours in my interests

Number Six: *The Questioner*

- [ ] I think rather than act
- [ ] I easily forget the good times
- [ ] I'm sometimes a rebel
- [ ] Leaders may have ulterior motives
- [ ] Once committed, I'm very loyal
- [ ] I sometimes feel unsafe
- [ ] I have a vivid imagination
- [ ] I often feel anxious
- [ ] I like being nonconformist
- [ ] I'm full of contradictions
- [ ] I can face danger
- [ ] I don't like getting things wrong
- [ ] It's hard to complete projects

- [ ] My failure is bigger than my success
- [ ] I'm suspicious of authority
- [ ] I support the underdog
- [ ] I don't like showing anger
- [ ] I like to question and doubt
- [ ] I expect the worst to happen
- [ ] I get involved in good causes
- [ ] I'm a responsible person
- [ ] I can be assertive and direct
- [ ] I often lose my confidence
- [ ] I am self-critical
- [ ] I have intellect and wit

Number Seven: *The Adventurer*

- [ ] I like excitement
- [ ] I enjoy making plans
- [ ] I feel good about myself
- [ ] I don't like being bored
- [ ] I can talk my way out of trouble
- [ ] I'm not good with depressed people
- [ ] I live life in the fast lane
- [ ] I put pleasure before hard work
- [ ] I'm an optimist
- [ ] I'm good at lots of things
- [ ] I'm not a good listener
- [ ] I usually get what I want
- [ ] I keep my options open
- [ ] I'm comfortable in social settings

- [ ] I don't have many problems
- [ ] I put painful things out of my mind
- [ ] I like to sample the best of life
- [ ] I like good, witty company
- [ ] Positive thinking solves problems
- [ ] I get over loss quicker than others do
- [ ] I have high ideals
- [ ] I don't like obligations
- [ ] I speak my mind
- [ ] I want both freedom and commitment
- [ ] I have many things on the go

Number Eight: *The Asserter*

- [ ] I like being in charge
- [ ] I have great energy for parties
- [ ] I don't trust others to be in charge
- [ ] Justice is important to me
- [ ] I sometimes go to excess
- [ ] I'm sometimes aggressive
- [ ] I respect people who stand up for themselves
- [ ] There's only one opinion: mine
- [ ] I don't hide my opinions
- [ ] I'm good at decision-making
- [ ] I work hard and get things done
- [ ] If I trust someone, I can be vulnerable
- [ ] I look for someone to blame

- [ ] Wrongdoers should be punished
- [ ] I defend the weak
- [ ] I get bored if there's no conflict or stimulation
- [ ] I am comfortable with anger
- [ ] I can be very blunt
- [ ] I don't like pretence
- [ ] I hate feeling dependent
- [ ] I see things in black and white
- [ ] I protect those I love
- [ ] I use anger and sex to make contact
- [ ] I like things to be very clear
- [ ] In a group I prefer to observe
- [ ] Middle ground: what's that?

Number Nine: *The Peacemaker*

☐ I leave important things until last

☐ It's hard to say 'no'

☐ Friends say I'm stubborn

☐ I don't easily express my anger

☐ I sense what others are feeling

☐ I like to be approved of

☐ I can spend hours on inessentials

☐ It's hard to know what I really want

☐ The past is very real to me

☐ All the Enneagram numbers describe me

☐ I can see all sides of the question

☐ I feel at one with people and nature

☐ It's hard to make decisions

☐ I live by familiar routines and habits

☐ I go along with what others suggest

☐ I don't often argue my position

☐ Other people's views are stronger than mine

☐ I often want to disobey the rules

☐ I enjoy just being with people

☐ I'm often thinking of many things at once

☐ I collect things

☐ Sometimes I come to a complete stop

☐ If I express my view I'll be abandoned

☐ It's hard to begin a job

☐ I'm good at supporting people

To be the best

Number One: *The Perfectionist*

*'I should be perfect; I should do the right thing.
And others should do so too.'*

As a One, your centre is
the gut or instinct,
and anger is a
core issue for
you: it only
seems right to get
angry when there is
a legitimate reason.

WHAT IS IT, DOC?

I'M AFRAID IT'S A HARDENING OF THE OUGHTERIES

What you avoid

You are likely to do your best to avoid anger, and find it hard
to recognize when you are angry.

— I CAN'T GO OUT TO PLAY–I'M HELPING IN THE HOME

The early years

*'As a child, I was criticized and
punished, so I made it my
business to be good.'*

*'I took on adult responsibility
early, and as far as possible
did nothing wrong.'*

*'I seem to have a critical voice
inside me which bombards me
with judgments.'*

GYM

FREE TIME?
WHAT'S THAT?

Ones at work

Ones enjoy jobs which involve detail and organization and which require self-discipline. They are good at bringing out the best in others and finding wise solutions to problems. Ones are often attracted to management, law enforcement, science, health care, education and accountancy. Many religious leaders are Ones. In their spare time, Ones often get involved in environmental and humanitarian causes or community work.

What's good and bad about being a One?

👍 reliable	👎 jealous
👍 honest	👎 inflexible
👍 productive	👎 critical
👍 wise	👎 judgmental
👍 strong vision	👎 dogmatic
👍 fair	👎 obsessive
👍 self-disciplined	👎 over-serious
👍 organized	👎 anxious
👍 efficient	👎 controlling
👍 principled	👎 resentful

Be good to yourself

☞ Each day, carve out time in your busy schedule to do something you really enjoy and which relaxes you.

☞ Question the critical voice inside you.

☞ Allow yourself to be less than perfect; it's good enough.

☞ Catch yourself thinking that there is only one answer. Try other people's solutions; they may be equally valid.

☞ Mind your language: change 'should' to 'want' or 'like'. So, 'We should have lunch' becomes 'I'd like to meet for lunch.' And don't suggest it if you don't want to.

☞ Learn how to tell jokes.

☞ Take yourself out for a treat – especially if you have left your room untidy!

☞ Make friends with anger, and discover if sadness or disappointment is lurking beneath it.

☞ Be proud, not critical, of what you have achieved.

☞ Praise others, even when you may also need to criticize them.

☞ Forgive yourself and others for faults and mistakes. We all fail sometimes.

Can I help you?
Number Two: *The Helper*

NO I'M FINE, REALLY I AM. HOW ARE YOU? HOW CAN I HELP?

'I need to be loved and appreciated, and to be free to express my feelings for others.'

As a Two, your centre is the heart or feelings. You tend to take on the feelings of others and be asleep to your own feelings.

You may show each of your friends a different self: Twos are concerned about how they come across to others.

What you avoid

You are likely to do your best to avoid being seen as needy, and to hide your 'unacceptable' side in order to be loved.

The early years

'As a child I felt I was loved for being helpful.'

DARLING YOU'RE SO HELPFUL AND GOOD. I COULDN'T MANAGE WITHOUT YOU- MY LOVELY LITTLE HELPER...

'I had to give emotional support to my parents. I find I am very sensitive to other people's needs.'

'I felt valued only for what I gave, and so now I make myself indispensable. That way, I get what I need in the way of appreciation without having to ask for it.'

Twos at work

Twos are often found in the helping professions and enjoy being associated with powerful people. They are attracted to jobs such as counselling, health care, acting and sales. In offices they are most likely to be the receptionist dealing with the public or the personal assistant supporting the important boss. The make-up artist or beauty therapist could well be a Two, satisfying the desire to create image but also to support. In their spare time, Twos often do voluntary work with underprivileged people.

I APPOINT YOU MY INDISPENSABLE HELPER, MY NUMBER TWO

JUST WHAT I WANT

What's good and bad about being a Two?

👍 caring

👍 able to detect others' moods

👍 unselfish

👍 altruistic

👍 gives unconditional love

👍 compassionate

👍 warm

👍 generous

👍 helpful

👍 encouraging

👎 easily hurt

👎 manipulates to be loved

👎 demands a response

👎 feels indispensable

👎 patronizing

👎 self-deceiving about motives

👎 domineering

👎 martyrlike

👎 feels a victim

👎 possessive

Be good to yourself

☞ Learn to do pleasurable activities on your own; you're worth it.

☞ Catch yourself manipulating or flattering; this stems from your anxiety to be loved.

☞ Choose to be with the person you like best, not the one who needs you most.

☞ Talk regularly about your inner life and your problems to someone you trust; it's all right to have your own needs.

☞ Practise saying 'no': 'I can't talk now,' or 'I can't help you.'

☞ Speak up if you feel you are being taken advantage of.

☞ Notice yourself swinging between feeling important and worthless. Learn your real value.

☞ Learn that people will still love you if you're independent.

☞ Avoid the hard-to-get relationship; this won't give you intimacy.

☞ Pay regular attention to yourself; go for a massage or a meal.

☞ Let someone else give to you – and enjoy it.

Close relationships

The Enneagram is not a matchmaking programme. It will not help you to find your ideal partner. But it will help you to understand yourself and your friends better, and it can help you to enjoy more fulfilling relationships.

This chapter takes a look at how the different personality types might handle close relationships. Find your number and see if it gives you some pointers towards the way you react to others. Don't forget to look also at the characteristics of the numbers on each side of you in the Enneagram drawing.

Number One: *The Perfectionist*

WHAT IF SHE DOESN'T LIKE MY TASTE IN SOFAS...?

One: 'I need to feel loved, even though I'm not perfect. I'm afraid you'll go away if I show my bad side or if I get angry. I'm glad that you can admit when you're wrong, because I find that hard to do.'

Partner: 'You have a great sense of humour, you're loyal and dedicated. But you can be critical. Please accept that I, too, am less than perfect.'

Number Two: *The Helper*

Two: 'I feel that I have to find a way of making you love me. I'm not sure you will love me for myself – whoever that is. So I will do what pleases you.'

I HOPE THESE WILL MAKE HIM STAY...

Partner: 'You make me feel special. You're generous and full of fun. But you have likes and dislikes too. Please let me see them. You don't have to manipulate me into loving you: I won't leave if you disagree with me or show your needs.'

Number Three: *The Achiever*

Three: 'I'll be whatever you want. You want 'sensitive'? You've got it. Don't ask me how I feel, though.'

HMM ~ WHICH ONE SHALL I WEAR TODAY?

Partner: 'You are responsible and generous, and I love your playfulness. But I'm not sure who the real you is. You're always performing, and your work often comes first. I want to know how you *feel*.'

Number Four: *The Romantic*

Four: 'I look forward to seeing you, and then find it hard to be 'present' when we're together. I feel I want something more, but I'm not sure what. I want to fathom the depths with you, but I'm scared you'll abandon me if I love you. I'm easily hurt, and I often feel jealous, moody and critical.'

COME CLOSER... NOT THAT CLOSE!

Partner: 'I love your sense of humour, your passion and your gentleness. And you understand me. But when we get close, you push me away.'

I LOVE YOU

ER... THERE'S THIS FASCINATING PROGRAMME ON...

Number Five: *The Observer*

Five: 'I keep deep feelings at bay when I'm with you; I somehow need to protect myself. But when I'm alone I think about you a lot.'

Partner: 'You are trustworthy and kind, and I find it easy to talk to you about things that bother me. But you withdraw when I get too close to you. I have to read between the lines to know if you like me.'

Number Six: *The Questioner*

Six: 'At last, I think I'm learning to trust you. I still feel more secure when *I'm* giving to *you*, though, because I'm not sure of your motives when you're giving to me.'

40TH ANNIVERSARY

YES, BUT DO YOU REALLY LOVE ME?

Partner: 'You have stuck by me through thick and thin. You're warm, fair and have a good sense of humour. But you can be sarcastic and controlling, and you withdraw when you feel insecure about me.'

Number Seven: *The Adventurer*

HEY- IT'S NOT SO BAD! LOOK AT THE MAGNIFICENT SCENERY!

Seven: 'I like it when we're having a good time together. I don't want to be with you when you're down; I want to distract you and make you feel happy again – or I'm out of here. Life is for enjoying!'

Partner: 'You are caring, generous and light-hearted. And you are great fun to be with – as long as we're doing the things we both enjoy and you don't have to listen to my problems.'

Number Eight: *The Asserter*

Eight: 'I love the intensity of the life we live together – the arguments, the passion. But I find it hard to let you in on the vulnerable person I am inside. I hate feeling dependent.'

– ALL I SAID WAS, "I'VE THROWN OUT YOUR OLD TRAINERS."

Partner: 'You are straight with me: loyal, caring and committed. But you're quick to find fault and slow to say sorry. I sometimes find your angry outbursts hard to bear. Be gentle: I won't see it as weakness.'

Number Nine: *The Peacemaker*

Nine: 'I want to become one with you, to merge with you. Your ways are my ways. I feel that if I try to pursue what *I* want, you will cease to love me.'

WE COULD BE HERE FOR HOURS

HERE THERE

WHICH WAY WOULD YOU LIKE TO GO?

I DON'T MIND WHICH WAY WOULD YOU LIKE TO GO?

Partner: 'You support me. You're kind, gentle and non-judgmental, and you understand my point of view. But I wish you'd say what *you* want sometimes: I'm not the only person in this relationship.'

Fifteen minutes of fame

Number Three: *The Achiever*

'I need to be productive
and successful, affirmed
and admired.'

As a Three, your centre
is the heart or feelings.
Interestingly, though,
Threes find it hard to know
exactly what they are feeling.

What you avoid

You are likely to do your best to avoid failure because you
are concerned to maintain your image.

The early years

'I was prized for my achievements.'

'The most common question my parents
asked was, "How well did you do?" '

'I felt it was important not to fail,
because only the winners were
worthy of being loved.'

'Our family was like the bouncy
family in the TV ad: superficial
activity and jollity, with no room
for deeper emotions.'

WHAT ARE YOU INTERESTED IN?

ANYTHING – AS LONG AS I'M IN THE PUBLIC EYE!

Threes at work

Threes work hard and enthusiastically. They are good at taking on authority and inspiring others, and they have boundless energy. Threes are often good at building up small businesses. They are attracted to jobs in advertising, sales and the media. They will often accept jobs where good promotion is offered. If they are politicians they will be the image-conscious ones, and if journalists, the high-powered ones.

What's good and bad about being a Three?

👍 authentic	👎 terrified of failure
👍 energetic	👎 calculating
👍 self-assured	👎 self-deceiving
👍 adaptable	👎 over-conscious of image
👍 possesses admired qualities	👎 self-promoting
👍 inner-directed	👎 arrogant
👍 efficient	👎 over-conscious of status
👍 industrious	👎 contemptuous
👍 popular	👎 competitive

Be good to yourself

☞ Go away for a weekend, leaving your work and your phone behind.

☞ To reduce stress, make time each day to meditate, have a long bath, listen to quiet music… or whatever relaxes you.

☞ As you slow down, don't run from the difficult feelings which may surface. Talk to someone about your vulnerabilities.

☞ Catch yourself postponing peace or happiness: 'When I've finished this project…' That moment never comes.

☞ Talk to someone about feeling a fraud: the difference you can see between your public image and private self.

☞ Begin to recognize what you feel by focusing on associated physical sensations such as a tense neck.

☞ Ask someone you trust to take you on a mystery trip and let them make all the decisions.

☞ Do some voluntary work; give because it's needed.

☞ Write time into your diary for seeing your partner and friends.

☞ Pay attention when a friend or partner needs to talk.

All heart

Number Four: *The Romantic*

I CAN'T GO OUT FEELING LIKE THIS...

'I need to be understood and to understand my own feelings.'

As a Four, your centre is the heart or feelings. Feelings feature large in your life and may at times be overwhelming.

What you avoid

You are likely to do your best to avoid being ordinary; you feel special, set apart from others.

The early years

'As a child, I felt abandoned. My mother looked to me for emotional support instead of the other way round.'

'I felt deprived, that I wasn't loved.'

'I felt I was only valued because I identified with my parents' troubles.'

'I felt a great sense of loss, as if nothing could ever fill the void.'

MUMMY'S SAD.

Fours at work

Fours are good at working with people in crisis. They can transform the ordinary into the extraordinary; and they look for authenticity and depth in any work that they do. They are good listeners; many choose counselling as a career. They enjoy work which allows them to search for depth and meaning in life, and make good psychologists. Many painters, writers, musicians and other artists are Fours. They are also attracted to teaching, and to the ritual side of religion.

What's good and bad about being a Four?

👍 sensitive

👍 sense of style

👍 creative

👍 intuitive

👍 self-revealing

👍 emotionally strong

👍 serious and funny

👍 self-aware

👍 warm

👍 aesthetically aware

👎 self-absorbed

👎 dark moods

👎 sense of despair and emptiness

👎 self-hating

👎 high expectations

👎 fear of abandonment

👎 feels there's never enough

👎 envious

Be good to yourself

☞ Mourn loss – it was real – then set it aside. This won't happen quickly or easily.

☞ When you're in a dark mood and self-absorbed, talk to a friend in order to shift your focus outwards.

☞ When feelings overwhelm you, tell yourself: 'This is not the whole story.'

☞ Complete the projects you begin; this has a beneficial effect.

☞ Concentrate on your present relationships instead of looking at past loss and abandonment.

☞ Catch yourself angling for special treatment by being difficult or eccentric.

☞ Don't reject what is easy to obtain; it may be very worthwhile.

☞ Your ability to empathize with others' pain is good and valuable; but their pain isn't yours, so learn to detach from it.

☞ Do regular physical exercise, preferably with others; this will help lighten your mood.

☞ Learn the hard lesson: 'What I have is enough. It only *feels* as if it isn't.'

I think, therefore I am
Number Five: *The Observer*

'I need to know everything and
to understand the world
around me. I want to be left
alone, to be self-sufficient.'

As a Five, your centre is the head or
thinking, and fear is a core issue for you. Fives are often afraid
to let themselves feel anything: it's safer to think than to feel.

What you avoid

You are likely to do your best to avoid being ignorant
or looking foolish.

The early years

'As a child, I felt intruded on.
They wanted access to my private
world, but I didn't want to let
them in.'

'It felt as if there was nobody
there for me, and so I learned
not to want anything: it was
too painful to want love and
not to get it.'

'I developed a whole world in
my head. I didn't need anything
or anybody else.'

Fives at work

Fives like intellectually demanding work, and many prefer to work on their own or at unsociable hours. They think clearly under pressure. They are attracted to science and technology, and anything that includes detailed analysis and problem-solving – sometimes the more obscure the better. They make very good counsellors. Many writers and artists are Fives, thriving on the isolated intensity and concentration required to pursue their art. Spare time occupations for Fives often include reading, stimulating discussions and working at their collections or personal projects.

THE NIGHT SHIFT

What's good and bad about being a Five?

👍 perceptive	👎 eccentric
👍 visionary	👎 deluded
👍 sensitive	👎 isolated
👍 focused	👎 cynical
👍 expert	👎 arrogant
👍 analytical	👎 paranoid
👍 original	👎 distant
👍 wise	👎 blinkered

Be good to yourself

☞ Risk expressing what you're thinking when you think it.

☞ Do something active each day as a change from thinking.

☞ Be spontaneous; go to the pub if invited.

☞ Catch yourself withdrawing when you're angry; instead, try to express your anger to the person concerned.

☞ Join a drama club, choir or art class to get more in touch with what your body can express.

☞ Notice when you retreat into analysing: are you escaping from a difficult emotion?

☞ Assess your deepest feelings: do they always lead to you being hurt?

☞ Notice the difference between how much you feel in private and how much you are able to feel in company.

☞ Give yourself treats: you are very used to doing without.

☞ Initiate a meeting with a trusted friend; this could be hard…

☞ Notice how much you think, 'I can do without you.'

☞ Be generous with your praise of others.

☞ Learn to experience life in the moment. Now is all we have.

Your spiritual self

If our relationships with each other are vitally linked to who we are and our personality type, so, too, is our spirituality. Our personalities will influence what we think about life, our purpose and the ways in which we relate to God. These insights may help you to develop the spiritual side of your nature.

It may be that your personality type is stuck in a particular way of thinking which prevents you from seeing the whole picture. Try completing the following statements according to what you have discovered about your personality. This may help you to see ways of thinking that you may be stuck in.

(Some examples are given.)

I am good because...

Threes ... I am successful.
Fives ... I am wise.
Sixes ... I am faithful.

In life I see only...

Ones ... imperfection.
Twos ... aching need.
Eights ... injustice and oppression.

I want...

Fours ... what others have got.
Sevens ... more of everything.
Nines ... to go to sleep.

Centring

Often if we want to pray or meditate we may find voices and distractions clamouring for our attention. Quietness is the last thing we experience. 'Centring' is all about finding a way to give our attention to that which is deeper than all the noise: to be able simply to 'be' with the reality of God.

The Enneagram indicates that the three centres – head, heart and gut – have different styles of centring and praying. But these are not fixed; there is always room to experiment and to find the style that suits you best.

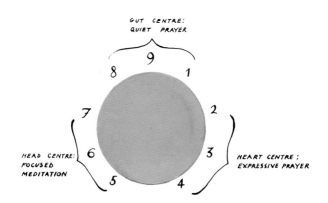

Some spiritual exercises

For Fives, Sixes and Sevens

You may be fearful that the world out there will knock you off-balance. Living as you do in your rich, often unfocused inner world, you need to find a way of restraining your natural desire to follow the many possibilities and ideas being suggested inside, and to be brought out into the world.

TRY THIS
Keep your eyes open and focus on an object which is significant for you, such as a candle or a cross. Gazing at a meaningful symbol can hold you in a focused state which may be impossible with your eyes closed. It is important that the object or symbol you choose is simple, or it may suggest thoughts and ideas which you find hard to resist. Use the same object each time you do this exercise.

For Twos, Threes and Fours

You may be continually affected by others' views and expectations. You struggle to be with and love yourself as you really are, and so in praying you need to find ways of exploring the dark places inside. The prospect of being alone and of beginning the inner journey can be frightening, and you need to learn to love yourself instead

TRY THIS
Close your eyes and listen to what is going on inside you. Look at your anger, anxiety, fears and joys; do not dismiss them. They are important and can lead you to see what is behind them. Listen for God's 'still small voice' which calls you to leave behind others' opinions, and to rest in your own truth and identity.

of looking outwards for approval from others. When the monsters in the dark have been named you can befriend them and harness them to give you creative energy.

For Eights, Nines and Ones

You may be full of energy and quick reactions. Aggression is part of your world and you have difficulty accepting affection. You need to find a way simply to be quiet in God's presence. An old man who spent hours praying each day was asked what he did all that time. He said, 'I don't do anything. I just look at God and God looks at me.' It may seem like time-wasting, but being silent in God's presence will help you to bring together your inner and outer worlds.

TRY THIS
Prepare for prayer by slowing down, perhaps by listening to music, or becoming aware of your breathing. Then direct your attention on God, 'desiring him for his own sake and not for his gifts… Do all in your power to forget everything else.' Distractions will come, but try using a short repeated word such as 'love' or 'God' to focus your mind, and refuse to develop any thoughts by arguing.

It's the time you have wasted for your rose that makes your rose so important.

43

The questioning mind

Number Six: *The Questioner*

'I need approval, and I need to feel I'm being taken care of. I question and I doubt.'

As a Six, your centre is your head or thinking, and fear is a core issue for you. Sixes are often suspicious of the intentions and motives of others. This is your way of coping with fear.

What you avoid

You are likely to do your best to avoid being seen as rebellious.

The early years

'I was afraid of the people who had power over me, and I never felt I could make my own decisions.'

'I never knew how my father was going to be from one day to the next. He was so unpredictable. I now find myself looking for a strong, trustworthy leader.'

'I was punished for acting against my parents. As an adult, I find it very hard to do what I want to do.'

Sixes at work

Sixes work best where there are clear lines of authority, and where the problems are defined. Some Sixes prefer a non-competitive environment, while other Sixes grasp their fear by the scruff of the neck and choose physical danger in their work. Sixes are attracted to the police or armed forces, law, business and academia. They make good team people and managers. Teaching and health care also suit them. Some choose to be self-employed in order to define their own lines of authority.

What's good and bad about being a Six?

👍 lovable	👎 indecisive
👍 committed	👎 cautious
👍 loyal	👎 defensive
👍 reliable	👎 controlling
👍 cooperative	👎 insecure
👍 self-affirming	👎 anxious
👍 compassionate	👎 unpredictable
👍 sense of humour	👎 self-defeating

Be good to yourself

☞ Don't be hard on yourself; accept that you have fears.

☞ Check to see if what you fear is actually there.

☞ Talk about your doubts in order to gain perspective on them.

☞ Ask for the guidelines to be made clear.

☞ Catch yourself watching for others to fulfil their promises.

☞ Choose to spend time with trustworthy and competent people.

☞ Stay in touch with people. If you withdraw, you can't accuse them of abandoning you.

☞ Build pleasurable, relaxing activities into your life.

☞ Believe people when they are affectionate and positive towards you.

☞ Give yourself approval instead of looking for it from others.

☞ Catch yourself remembering only the negative things.

☞ There are many 'right' directions to take. Learn to be comfortable with the choice you make.

☞ Notice that the world doesn't end when you make a mistake.

Sevens just want to have fun

Number Seven: *The Adventurer*

*'I need to plan to have fun, to be happy
and to contribute to the world.'*

As a Seven, your centre
is your head or thinking,
and fear is a core issue
for you. Your way of
coping with fear is
to bury it by pursuing
pleasant options and
by going after more
of everything.

COME ON—LET'S
GO TO THE
NEXT PARTY!

What you avoid

You are likely to do your best to avoid anxiety, suffering
and pain.

The early years

MORE, DADDY MORE!

*'I was afraid, so I escaped into an
imaginary world.'*

*'I can't remember any feelings of
hate or blame from my childhood.
I concentrate on the good things,
the best times.'*

*'I think I'm a bit of a Peter Pan —
an eternal child.'*

Sevens at work

Sevens are good at brainstorming, networking, bringing together opposing ideas and introducing lightness into a difficult situation. They can work hard for good causes, and enjoy varied, stimulating work. They are ideas people and plan well. They can make good writers or editors, and are particularly good at storytelling. Sevens often choose work which involves travelling: as pilots, flight attendants or journalistic photographers, for example. Sevens can be attracted to daring pursuits such as skydiving and rock climbing. They have active social lives, and fitness and healthy eating can be priorities for them.

What's good and bad about being a Seven?

👍		👎	
👍 appreciative		👎 greedy for experience	
👍 responsive		👎 hyperactive	
👍 vivacious		👎 superficial	
👍 productive		👎 materialistic	
👍 uninhibited		👎 never satisfied	
👍 gets things done		👎 self-centred	
👍 optimistic		👎 out of control	
👍 generous		👎 uncommitted	

Be good to yourself

☞ Recognize that age and maturity have equal value to youth and energy.

☞ Talk to a trusted friend about something that is bothering you.

☞ When you're in overdrive, stop and take stock. Are you running away from something?

☞ Try focusing on one activity or person for longer than normal, without jumping to the next thing.

☞ Don't be afraid to go below the surface in your relationships; depth and commitment bring much pleasure.

☞ Take other people's concerns seriously.

☞ Develop the ability to stay with the present moment; get beyond the boredom threshold.

☞ Charm is good, but recognize when you're using it to hide a problem.

☞ Catch yourself feeling anxious when your options are limited: learn to be content with what's available.

☞ Don't make light of your own problems; they are real.

I did it my way!

Number Eight: *The Asserter*

'I need to be self-reliant and strong, to make an impact on the world. I like having power over others.'

HMM. SO SHE'S LEFT ME ... ON WITH THE PARTY

As an Eight, your centre is the gut or instinct, and anger is a core issue for you. You have no difficulty in expressing anger.

What you avoid

You are likely to do your best to avoid being seen as weak.

The early years

'If I cried when I was hurt, I was ridiculed. I had to stand up for myself and not show any weakness.'

'I grew up in the inner city where gangs and bullying were the norm. It was a case of winning fights or not surviving.'

NO, NO IT DOESN'T HURT AT ALL – I'M O.K.

'I don't show my limitations, or let on when I'm hurt, physically or emotionally.'

Eights at work

Eights are good at taking on huge projects and moving them forward at the right pace. They prefer to be leaders than to be led, and can have a strong instinct for fairness and justice, especially in protecting the innocent. Eights are often self-employed. In the business world they would either be the entrepreneur or the powerful executive. Law attracts them, as does leadership in trade unions. If they are politicians they will use their power with fairness. In health care they will be the consultant, the professor or the dedicated health manager. Eights are also suited to the competitive nature of the sports profession.

What's good and bad about being an Eight?

👍 good leader

👍 courageous

👍 self-confident

👍 inspirational

👍 authoritative

👍 protective

👍 honourable

👍 entrepreneurial

👍 enjoys life

👍 independent

👎 aggressive

👎 domineering

👎 empire-building

👎 dictatorial

👎 bullying

👎 wilful

👎 vengeful

👎 possessive

👎 blaming

👎 controlling

Be good to yourself

☞ You develop trust through sparring; recognize that this may not be how others develop trust.

☞ Try letting someone else in your team initiate action.

☞ Catch yourself wanting to break the rules.

☞ When you feel bored, recognize that this could be masking a deeper emotion.

☞ Your excesses – drinking, socializing and so on – are replacing something you really want. Join a self-help group if necessary.

☞ Try compromising now and again; you may find that your 'enemies' become friends as you enter the middle ground.

☞ Count to ten before letting out your anger.

☞ Try admitting you're wrong every now and then.

☞ Don't dismiss the experience and views of other people; they are as valid as yours.

☞ Praise people as much as you can.

☞ Try and see how your directness may intimidate.

☞ If you're hurt, express this sooner rather than later.

☞ Talk about your anger with someone you trust.

☞ Have fun with people who enjoy your outrageousness.

☞ Spend time with those who are equally direct and honest.

Blessed are the peacemakers

Number Nine: *The Peacemaker*

> *'I need to keep the peace
> and to merge with others.
> I want to preserve things
> as they are.'*

WHAT IS IT DOC?

HMM - I'D SAY IT WAS SHAKING HANDS. CUT DOWN ON BEING NICE TO PEOPLE

As a Nine, your centre is the
gut or instinct, and anger is a
core issue for you. You find it
hard to get in touch with your anger;
it is as if it has gone to sleep.

What you avoid

You are likely to do your best to avoid conflict; 'peace at
any price' could be your motto.

SHOUT
ORDER
ARGUE
OPINION
ANT
GRR...
I WANT

The early years

*'As a child, I felt overlooked.
My opinions or feelings weren't
important.'*

*'I was caught between my
siblings and my parents.
I had to keep the peace by going
along with their wishes.'*

*'I find it hard to say 'no' or to
know what I really want or feel,
because I never got used to listening to my own voice.'*

Nines at work

Nines are good at giving unwavering support, and thrive in situations where there is a clear course of action, with no need to make continuing decisions. Because they are good at identifying with other opinions, they make good mediators and diplomats. Some are happy in jobs that contain a lot of routine and protocol, such as the armed forces or the civil service. Other Nines are attracted to the helping professions: nursing, social work, counselling, dentistry. In general, they are comfortable with work that involves organization and detail.

WELL, WHAT DO YOU THINK ABOUT THAT IDEA?

What's good and bad about being a Nine?

👍 contented	👎 unreflective
👍 self-possessed	👎 passive
👍 unselfconscious	👎 indecisive
👍 optimistic	👎 complacent
👍 supportive	👎 fatalistic
👍 patient	👎 obstinate
👍 good-humoured	👎 self-effacing
👍 peaceful	👎 forgetful
👍 perceptive	👎 repressed

Be good to yourself

☞ Catch yourself depending on other people to make your decisions.

☞ When you're weighing up the pros and cons, ask yourself how you *feel*.

☞ Make a clear plan for yourself when you begin a project.

☞ Try stating your own opinions; others will value them.

☞ Don't just listen to problems; share your own, too.

☞ Try saying 'no' to at least one inessential thing each day.

☞ Finish one project before starting on the next.

☞ Learn that it's all right to have the attention focused on you.

☞ Trust your gut feelings about a choice you're making.

☞ Make choices by eliminating what you don't want.

☞ When you overdose on food, television and so on, try to look at the feelings you're hiding.

☞ Try writing the really urgent letter before clearing your desk.

☞ Notice your stubbornness when pushed.

☞ Don't see anger as an enemy; use it to spur you into action.

☞ Build physical exercise into your weekly routine.

☞ Realize that you don't have to fulfil everyone's expectations.

Only one number?

In the Enneagram your personality type is not limited to one number plus varying amounts of your 'wings' – the numbers on each side of you. There is a lot of movement. You do not change your number, but in differing circumstances and moods you can move towards or experience the characteristics – both positive and negative – of the two other numbers you are linked to by the lines on the Enneagram drawing.

When you are feeling secure, you may take on the positive qualities of either of these numbers. When you are under stress, you may take on their negative qualities. You are still the same you, but you can find yourself thinking and behaving differently depending on how secure or stressed you feel. The more aware you are of what is happening within you, the more choice you will have about the way you live.

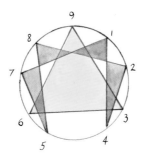

Number One: *The Perfectionist*

Moving towards Number Seven: *The Adventurer*

When you move towards the positive side of Number Seven, you may become:
   more self-accepting
   more optimistic
   more spontaneous
   better able to focus on good rather than bad things
   better able to enjoy for enjoyment's sake

When you move towards the negative side of Number Seven, you may become:
   self-destructive through excess: drugs, alcohol and so on

Moving towards Number Four: *The Romantic*

When you move towards the positive side of Number Four, you may become:
   better able to experience deeper feelings
   more likely to enjoy creative activities

When you move towards the negative side of Number Four, you may become:
   indignant at unmet expectations
   depressed, turning your anger inwards
   prone to feeling unloved or unlovable
   subject to a sense of longing for the unattainable

Number Two: *The Helper*

Moving towards Number Four: *The Romantic*

When you move towards the positive side of Number Four, you may become:
   more willing to admit to painful feelings
   better at saying 'no'
   able to find self-worth by other means than helping others
   more comfortable with being alone
   better able to express creativity

When you move towards the negative side of Number Four, you may become:
    self-absorbed and depressed
    prone to lamenting your failure compared to others

Moving towards Number Eight: *The Asserter*

When you move towards the positive side of Number Eight, you may become:
    more self-confident
    more honest and straightforward
    less concerned for approval

When you move towards the negative side of Number Eight, you may become:
    less kind, loving or trusting
    harder and more isolated
    more demanding and ambitious to take charge
    more irritable and critical

Number Three: *The Achiever*

Moving towards Number Six: *The Questioner*

When you move towards the positive side of Number Six, you may become:
    more committed to your closest family and friends
    better able to look for what is best in others
    more in touch with your own feelings
    better able to be vulnerable

When you move towards the negative side of Number Six, you may become:
    fearful of being rejected
    dependent and anxious
    unable to make decisions

Moving towards Number Nine: *The Peacemaker*

When you move towards the positive side of Number Nine, you may become:
    more relaxed and peaceful
    more receptive
    able to have a broader view of life

When you move towards the negative side of Number Nine, you may become:
   indecisive and apathetic
   prone to neglecting your own welfare
   less productive
   resentful of anyone who points out your shortcomings

Number Four: *The Romantic*

Moving towards Number One: *The Perfectionist*

When you move towards the positive side of Number One, you may become:
   more self-disciplined
   more practical
   more positive
   better able to act on your principles
   less controlled by your feelings

When you move towards the negative side of Number One, you may become:
   critical and angry
   moralizing
   subject to guilt at failure

Moving towards Number Two: *The Helper*

When you move towards the positive side of Number Two, you may become:
   better able to connect meaningfully with others
   more healthily detached from others
   less self-absorbed

When you move towards the negative side of Number Two, you may become:
   prone to manipulating others into loving you
   prone to repressing your own needs
   increasingly dependent
   prone to becoming ill to attract attention

Number Five: *The Observer*

Moving towards Number Eight: *The Asserter*

When you move towards the positive side of Number Eight, you may become:
    better able to move from thought to action
    more spontaneous
    more assertive
    energized by your anger, instead of withdrawing

When you move towards the negative side of Number Eight, you may become:
    punitive
    prone to acting unreasonably
    prone to ignoring others' feelings blatantly rather than secretly

Moving towards Number Seven: *The Adventurer*

When you move towards the positive side of Number Seven, you may become:
    able to experience life more broadly
    less self-conscious
    less inhibited

When you move towards the negative side of Number Seven, you may become:
    impulsive about taking on new projects
    distracted

Number Six: *The Questioner*

Moving towards Number Nine: *The Peacemaker*

When you move towards the positive side of Number Nine, you may become:
    better able to empathize with others
    able to take a broader view of life
    less serious and more energetic
    able to trust your own inner authority

When you move towards the negative side of Number Nine, you may become:
    unable to act, apathetic
    prone to using drugs, television, food and so on as a distraction

Moving towards Number Three: *The Achiever*

When you move towards the positive side of Number Three, you may become:
    more decisive
    better able to take effective action
    better able to see the good in your efforts

When you move towards the negative side of Number Three, you may become:
    busy to avoid anxiety
    afraid of failing, so that you stick to familiar things
    prone to taking on a role in order to feel secure
    prone to lying to get ahead or cover up

Number Seven: *The Adventurer*

Moving towards Number Five: *The Observer*

When you move towards the positive side of Number Five, you may become:
    quieter and more objective
    better able to value wisdom, self-discipline and being serious
    better able to accept bad things as well as good
    better able to look at your own fears

When you move towards the negative side of Number Five, you may become:
    more likely to theorize
    self-absorbed
    prone to escaping from your responsibilities

Moving towards Number One: *The Perfectionist*

When you move towards the positive side of Number One, you may become:
    better able to make things happen
    more interested in the welfare of others
    better able to consider options wisely

When you move towards the negative side of Number One, you may become:
   cynical and nit-picking
   unable to laugh at yourself
   convinced that you know the truth
   prone to blaming others for spoiling your fun
   obsessed by an idea

Number Eight: *The Asserter*

Moving towards **Number Two**: *The Helper*

When you move towards the positive side of Number Two, you may become:
   more open and vulnerable
   more concerned for the welfare of others
   more loving and lovable
   better able to express your softer side

When you move towards the negative side of Number Two, you may become:
   over-dependent
   prone to placing unrealistic demands on others
   defensive and likely to over-react

Moving towards **Number Five**: *The Observer*

When you move towards the positive side of Number Five, you may become:
   more objective
   better able to think before acting

When you move towards the negative side of Number Five, you may become:
   withdrawn and less active
   less in touch with your own feelings
   prone to fearing rejection from others
   depressed
   subject to feelings of guilt

Number Nine: *The Peacemaker*

Moving towards Number Three: *The Achiever*

When you move towards the positive side of Number Three, you may become:
    more efficient and productive
    able to develop a sharper focus
    more self-confident
    better able to take control of your life

When you move towards the negative side of Number Three, you may become:
    prone to taking on too much
    prone to working in order to get approval
    prone to trying to impress

Moving towards Number Six: *The Questioner*

When you move towards the positive side of Number Six, you may become:
    more direct
    more loyal
    more practical

When you move towards the negative side of Number Six, you may become:
    overwhelmed by worry
    self-doubting and rigid
    passive and apathetic

Taking it further

If this book has given you a taste for using the Enneagram to find out more about yourself and others, there are various paths you can pursue.

It is helpful to join a group working on the Enneagram if you can, because it gives you a chance to compare your experience with others with the same personality type as yours, and to hear what people who have different personality types say about their experiences. The group can also give support and acceptance when uncomfortable things come to the surface, as they inevitably will. Look at the journal *Retreats* for details of Enneagram retreats. You could also contact retreat leaders to find out about other possibilities.

There are a number of books on the Enneagram that may help you, and below are listed the ones that I have found useful. You will also find many more listed in Internet bookshops.

Retreats, National Retreat Association, The Central Hall, 256 Bermondsey Street, London SE1 3UJ; tel: 0171 3577736

Enneagram Spirituality: From compulsion to contemplation
ISBN 0-87793-471-1 (hardback) or 0-87793-466-5 (paperback), Suzanne Zuercher, copyright © 1992 Ave Maria Press, Notre Dame Indiana 46556, USA

The Enneagram and Prayer: Discovering our true selves before God
ISBN 0-87193-259-8, copyright © 1987 Barbara Metz and Jon Burchill, published Dimension Books Inc., Denville, New Jersey 07834, USA

The Enneagram Made Easy: Discover the 9 types of people
ISBN 0-06-251026-6, copyright © 1994 Renee Baron and Elizabeth Wagele, published HarperCollins Publishers, 10 East 53rd Street, New York, NY 10022, USA

The Enneagram: Understanding yourself and the others in your life
ISBN 0-06-250683-8, Helen Palmer, copyright © 1988 Center for the Investigation and Training of Intuition, published HarperCollins Publishers, 10 East 53rd Street, New York, NY 10022, USA

Personality Types: Using the Enneagram for self-discovery
ISBN 0-85030-744-9, copyright © 1987 Don Richard Riso, published Aquarian HarperCollins Publishers, 77–85 Fulham Palace Road, Hammersmith, London W6 8JB